Wit Snark and Light in the Dark

Also by Deborah Smith Parker

Humanus Astrologicus
The Horse that Haunts My Heart

Wit, Snark and Light in the Dark

Deborah Smith Parker

TOP READS PUBLISHING, LLC

Vista, California USA

Copyright © 2022 by Deborah Smith Parker

All Rights Reserved. No part of this publication may be reproduced, stored in or introduced into a retrieval system, or transmitted in any form or by any means (electronic, mechanical, photocopied, recorded of otherwise), without the prior written permission of both the copyright owner and the publisher of this book, except by a reviewer who wishes to quote brief passages in connection with a review written for insertion in a magazine, newspaper, broadcast, website, blog or other outlet.

First Edition

ISBN: 978-1-970107-02-9 (paperback)
ISBN: 978-1-970107-31-9 (ebook)

Library of Congress Control Number:

Wit, Snark, and Light in the Dark is published by:
Top Reads Publishing, LLC
1035 E. Vista Way, Suite 205
Vista, CA 92084 USA

For information please direct emails to:
info@topreadspublishing.com

Cover design, book layout and typography: Teri Rider & Associates
Author photo: Alex Slattery, https://wabisabifoto.com/

Printed in the United States of America

Dedication

For Mary Steussy Shanahan, PhD., who dedicated her life to her love of literature, her students and her husband and family.

Contents

Foreword xiii
Free Verse 1
Romantic Nonsense Deconstructed 3
First Magic 4
Stingy Little Gods 5
How I Got Lost from Where I was Going 6
Rusty Chevrolet 8
Some Thoughts on Turning 65 9
Epigrams 11
Ancient Curse 12
It is Written 14
Discount Buying Fever 16
A Midwesterner's Lament 18
Biostitute 19
They Let Caltrans* Out Today 20
To My Friends Leaving California for Simpler Places . 22
I Want to Go Home 23
What's Wrong with These Pictures? 25
Cappuccino by the Sea 27
Drug *Du Jour* 30
Everybody was Surprised 31
We Women will Take Charge from Here 36
Kill for Christ 38
Beacon 39

The Craftsman 39
Wake Up! 40
Armor 41
If You and I were Angels 42
I Write 43
Lovely Death 44
Grief 45
The Question 47
Splendor 47
Mortal Remains 48
Strange Customs 49
A Season Short of Time 50
Magic 51
Legacy 53
The Serpent's Embrace 54
First Sacred Fire 55
Where Two or More are Gathered 56
Beltane's Embers 57
Star Catcher 60
Science Wasn't There That Night 61
Star Pools 62
The Visit 63
Guardianship of the Light 65
I'd Like to Know 67
Wags 72
Low, Slow Fire 73
Qlippoth* 74

Heliotropism 75
It's a Stretch with Beagles 75
Kitchen Helpers 76
Double-shot Ambience. 77
Come on Down the Road 80
Prayer of a Communicant 81
The Canoe 84
Through Eyes About to Die 85
When I am Old 90
The Temple 93
About the Author. 101

Foreword

By Claudia Black, Ph.D.

I have been reading Deborah Parker's poems for more than three decades. Each piece I read, regardless of form or subject matter, leaves me in awe of how she is able to speak both to the conscious and unconscious within us, helping to better see their connections. I marvel at how frequently Deborah's work moves me into contemplative states, depths I hadn't yet touched, releasing tears I hadn't realized were there. Or so tickled that I laugh out loud.

I feel her writing speaks not just to the heart in us but the soul, coaxing out long forgotten or buried memories, some filled with delight, others spiked with pain. She draws out family dynamics and other relationships with both wit and struggle, driven by the push and pull needed for resolving these internal and very human conflicts. Life passages with their accompanying denial and insights leading to release are common themes. Her images are profound and her rhythms navigate us to new depth and clarity.

As an internationally recognized psychotherapist, author and speaker, my work is credited with contributing significantly to paving the way for others to incorporate an educational framework and therapeutic direction to identify and heal the impact of impaired family dynamics, childhood trauma, and internal conflicts. What I know and have witnessed is that well-crafted poetry and prose—especially evident in Deborah's works—offer great healing to the wounded heart, seeding the growth of resilience. Such writing resonates with that part of the brain that stores life's struggles, and in doing so offers hope that comes with validation from a depth not usually reached when one just has face-to-face conversations.

As you read you will enter Deborah's world of well-crafted observations, experiences, and lessons learned and offered ranging from lifestyle, family history, challenges of day to day busyness and her often unique commentary on the effects of our contacts with non-material worlds. You will find her poems allow you to pause your busy life, your busy brain so you may consider what is truly important to you. I suspect Deborah's writings will nudge and even push you, as they have me, to reflect on what has occurred in your life to review what you need to release, and what you want to embrace and perpetuate. And you get to do this through the many examples of Deborah's keen knowledge of archetypes, her acute inner perceptions and absorption of life going on around and through her, her passion for social justice, and most importantly her incredible heart.

It is my honor and privilege to introduce you to Deborah's poems contained in this book. I hope they will speak to you as they have spoken to me, spotlighting elements that embrace the complexity, pain, humor and joy of being human.

Claudia Black, Ph.D., is an addiction and trauma expert and has authored 16 books on the subject. Her seminal work, *It Will Never Happen to Me*, would pull the covers off the "no talk" rules about addiction and abuse. Her latest book is *Unspoken Legacy*. Claudia's website is www.claudiablack.com.

Free Verse

I chafe against this modern curse
that poetry is now free verse,
a cultural dark indicator
that depression is now greater
than at any time preceding.
Inwardly our souls are bleeding.

Out across the page words ooze
any way the poets choose,
shunning classic formal orders
and more tightly laid-out borders,
stating every slight and sin
with very little discipline.

When I'm filled with raging fire
or I've lost some heart's desire,
I don't go wandering about
and leave my punctuation out
or think big problems I'll efface
by stating them in lower case.

My words are not out running loose;
I tie them up with metric noose.
Conjuring old paradigms

I weave the lines with modern rhymes
so no one has to scratch her head
and wonder what the hell I've said.

If art as verse is truly free
there should be room for those like me.

Romantic Nonsense Deconstructed

When Wordsworth wrote we're "trailing clouds
of glory" from whence we all came,
he'd never met the hordes and crowds
of those who've borne my family name.

When Byron claimed a woman's love
was the all of her existence,
he didn't clarify the dove
was so caged by men's insistence.

When Keats said all we need to know
is truth is beauty, he was wrong.
Perhaps he only thought it so
because he didn't live too long.

Those agents Coleridge would use
to call his muse into accord
would other minds twist and confuse
and end them up at Betty Ford.

Their impress should not be belied,
nor how on art they gave instruction.
Perhaps it's good that they all died
before the time of deconstruction.

First Magic

The magic of stories,
first drawn
in my imagination
by the voices of my parents:

My mother's voice
flowed under me,
gently bubbling water
tumbling from the pages
of many wondrous books
and I would float all warm
in her circling currents.

My father's voice
stole thunder from the heavens
to tell of times when gods
first climbed down from the stars
to face us on the same field of battle,
and forever woke those gods
who slept inside of me.

Stingy Little Gods

The great gods are all dead.
Religion killed them,
religion and its stingy little gods
who stole their worshippers.
(That's how you kill a god.)

The great ones now are banished
to darkness
as faint pictures in the stars
too far away for most,
but their dim shapes in the night sky
still hold the magic
my father told me stories about
when I was little.

The stingy little gods
don't like magic,
and their followers will hunt you and hurt you
if you look anywhere other
than where the little gods point.

How I Got Lost from Where I Was Going

I loved to write with pen in hand
but then was forced to understand
and learn the ways technology,
through agency of my PC,
transformed the ways I must compose.
Computers take me to new lows.
My input gets so far afield
quickly and can bring strange yield
like what occurred the other day
and which to you I'll now convey.

I thought I'd typed out "supersede."
Imagine my surprise, indeed,
when in the draft I'd typed and read
glowed "suKPERSED" on my screen instead.
It looked a little bit obscene
glaring at me from my screen.
Confused at first I quickly solved
just how "suKPERSED" had evolved.

My right-hand rests upon the "L"
which causes me this endless hell.
My hand was one key off that day.
Instead of "L" I got a "K,"

and while on this keyboard spree
my left hand hit the "Caps Lock" key.
Not only did I lose home base
now everything was uppercase.
I don't know why it ends with "D,"
I guess I just forgot the "E."

But good old spellcheck with my Word
did not find "suKPERSED" too absurd.
Sure, it said, "suKPERSED not found,"
but then the choices did abound
and what was first and in the lead
but what I'd intended, "supersede."
From that point on then life seemed grand
'cause spell check seemed to understand
with wisdom all so full of knowing
how I got lost from where I was going.

Rusty Chevrolet

I drive the information highway in my rusty Chevrolet
of a 1940s vintage and in it I will stay.
I do not know nor do I care just how the darn thing works
so I really start to panic when it stalls and shows its quirks.
On the information highway I use only lower gears,
and when others speed on by me I just ignore their jeers.

A committed back roads traveler, I do not want to change
my vehicle or route for expansion of my range.
This sleek new highway system has so many intersections
that I'm always getting lost and have to stop to ask directions.
But chugging up the on-ramp there is one thing that I know—
on the information highway I can always get a tow.

Some Thoughts on Turning 65

Some thoughts on turning 65:
The first one is I'm still alive!
There were times that's been in doubt
but so far everything's worked out.

Twenty five years now have passed
since I wore my bikini last.
My slutty black dress days are gone.
At 9:00 p.m. I start to yawn.

My ears now have a frequent buzz.
I'm one breast lighter than I was.
The one that's left is getting saggy;
the skin below my eyes is baggy.

My back's not stooped and I don't wheeze
but there's this thing about my knees,
like when I get down on the floor
which I don't do much anymore.

So who's this woman that I see
each morning looking back at me?
Not the one who caught men's glances,
causing them to make advances.

65! It can't be true!
My mother is the person who
is 65 not me, no way!
When DID these wrinkles come to stay?

I moisturize but can't escape
how my skin's morphed into crepe.
But even though kids call me ma'am
I'm more at ease with who I am.

Although my body has declined
I love what's happened with my mind.
This consciousness that I've collected
is put to good use, is respected.

I'm driven more to find life's wonder;
I mind much less now when I blunder
because I'm called to risk, explore
a lot more than I did before.

Epigrams

The inspiration of each breath
to live just brings us nearer death.

* * * * * * *

A union forged and filled by sex
just generates two hollow wrecks.

* * * * * * *

Anglers cast out bait for fish
to bite, so each may get his wish.

* * * * * * *

Oh, Freedom, how you do enslave;
You are unkind and so unjust
to make the smoothest way to pave
my way is do the things I must.

Ancient Curse

We poets tend to render less
from ecstasy than tenderness.
By tenderness I mean intense,
but soft, compression of immense.
By ecstasy I mean the kind
more physical and less of mind.
We question if there is as much
in each caress and urgent touch
as in the light an image brings
from which a living poem springs.

As fated poets we don't choose
who or what will be our muse.
Our ethereally tuned receivers
make us destined image weavers
driven by a grand desire
not to act but to inspire.

Inheritors of ancient curse
we transform images to verse
from phantom forms that roil behind
those veils which often keep us blind,
that press our fingers to explore
just how our words can find the door

and more importantly, the key,
to spring those captive shadows free.

If sleight of hand could bring forth words
as stage magicians do with birds,
we still would choose our poet's hell
ensconced in its psychotic cell.
There's purpose to the way we brood—
it helps to get us in the mood
to tormentedly explore
those junctures others just ignore.

It is Written

I argued with this scientist,
a learned man was he;
he wagged his finger, shook his fist
at my astrology.

He was such a brilliant sort
with three advanced degrees.
Academics weren't my forte;
I drank, got B's and C's.

He said, "There is no fate in life,
we exercise free choice.
We create the good or strife."
(He really raised his voice.)

I had snapped this verbal bait,
swallowed not just bitten.
"All I'd like to say is 'fate
is anything that's written.' "

He snorted: "Nothing's cast in stone,
no obstacle too high.
Adversity is overcome
by those who really try."

Well, neither of us got our way
in those intense frenetics.
And, oh, did I neglect to say
his specialty? Genetics.

Discount Buying Fever

Discount fever sweeps our land
and clearly has the upper hand.
Drawn like lemmings to the sea
to ugly warehouses go we
to flock through airplane hangar doors
to chilly, drafty gray decors.

Industrial size unit measures
just hyperbolize our pleasures.
We're all volume buyers now
buying half a side of cow.
Through stacks of cartons we will sort
to buy our Advil by the quart,
mayonnaise in five-gallon jars,
ten-pound drums of candy bars,
ripened berries by the flat,
chocolate syrup by the vat,
peanut butter by the barrel,
deals on stacks of new apparel,
toilet paper piled on pallets,
a year's supply of fresh-picked shallots!
There for any willing taker—
carpeting sold by the acre,
deals on crates of wine and beer,
how will we get this out of here?

Is there precedent in history
or is this a New Age mystery?
How did the mighty line of Caesars
store much booty without freezers?
Did Attila stand an hour
in line to buy his tons of flour
to keep his troops fed while they'd pillage
every European village?
Our gene pool's thinned, we queue like sheep
to checkers in lines thirteen deep.
We don't dwell on conquering Rome,
just how to get the darned stuff home.

A Midwesterner's Lament

It's spring in California,
finally, I'm learning—
the grass is turning brown
and the hills have started burning.

It's spring in California
when each concrete river bed
carries tumbleweeds and dust
and all the wildflowers are dead.

Yes, it's spring in California,
at last I now can tell;
and they say we don't have seasons—
which is also true of hell.

Biostitute

Did it come from planned intent
or was it purely accident
that the word "biostitute"
rhymes perfectly with prostitute?

They Let Caltrans* Out Today
Day in the Life of a Southern California Commuter

This morning I left Thousand Oaks
along with other hopeful folks
to make the drive down 101
toward L.A. and the rising sun,
heading into traffic mayhem
of rush hour in the L.A. a.m.
Squinting into smog and glare
I thought it best to say a prayer:
"Oh, please make this a lovely day
and don't let Caltrans out today."

At the Calabasas grade
I knew it futile that I'd prayed.
In lanes where traffic should be streaming
stood Caltrans workers staring, dreaming,
huddled with their pavement breakers
and other dust and noisemakers
while scratching noses, other parts
as crew chiefs check their reams of charts.
Another crushing, long delay
'cause they let Caltrans out today.

Thinking I'd be clever and cute
I took a chance on one more route,
so I cut down through Malibu
and sure enough I found a crew
of Caltrans workers who had set
five miles of orange cones out and yet
were doing nothing I could tell
but backing traffic up like hell.
Is there some bureaucrat to pay
to not let Caltrans out today?

California State Department of Transportation

To My Friends Leaving California for Simpler Places

Those epicurean delights
of San Diego's balmy nights—
that's in the past, forget it fast.
You're going where there's bland repast.
Since you're moving someplace rural
I hope that you like squirrel
 or buffalo or moose meat—
better yet some duck or goose feet.

Here on sushi you can dine
or sweet morsels braised in wine.
There your choices will be few
and you'd kill for something new
or else be close to suicide
when served another meal that's fried.
Out there to get a tasty thrill
they just go wild and pour on dill!

I know I sound contrary,
but there the menus seldom vary
and the only part that wavers
is the different Jell-O flavors.
You don't think I'm being fair?
Please listen, friend. I came from there.

I Want to Go Home

I want to go home
and leave this brown dry place with its concrete rivers
where only a few respect nature's cycles and strange trees
grow 20 feet in one year.

I want to go home
and dig my bare feet and hands in deep black soil that
grows corn and alfalfa in the humid sunshine near rich
arrays of lilacs, wild violets, and swaths of Queen Anne's
lace that only briefly bloom between the bitter winters.

I want to go home
to new snow with dazzling, brilliant colors and old
snow, crusty, dirty, creating a suicidal state in me lasting
through March when I can once more roll like a pig in
the incredible intoxication that follows each spring when
sap rises in all living things.

I want to go home
to a time when my parents were young and could do
magical things and didn't need the care I give them now.

I want to go home
because I'm in another crisis of direction and need all
the help I can get from my foundations, even if they are
missing a few key pieces.

I want to go home
though I would be leaving what I sought all my life and
left home to find.

What's Wrong With These Pictures?

I love those outdoor catalogues although I find it odd
that they all project an image of some movie set facade.
The layouts hint of camping, the sellers hope you buy it,
but it really looks to me as if they're camping at the Hyatt.

Something critical is missing from each Pima cotton shirt,
so what's wrong with these pictures? They never show us dirt.
The photos that they staged for each upscale catalogue
were surely never taken after portage through a bog.

No one's posed in old canoes parked on some beaver dam
eating sandwiches of Rye Krisp and cold and slimy Spam.
They're never shown in clothes with rips nor look like
    they perspire,
and pictures never show them fishing dinner from the fire.

That shiny, glossy cookware with its black enamel sheen
that was featured in a special on a page from L.L. Bean
never seems to show the crust and other kinds of crud
from being washed in rivers and scrubbed with gritty mud.

Have you noticed that the models from Land's End and
    Eddie Bauer
always have such happy faces, they never seem to glower?

Their sleeping bags were never wet, those people look
 carefree;
they're never shown in shoulder sling from chopping
down some tree.

Models bask in bug-less paradise, they never gasp or cough
'cause some mosquito-crazed companion sprayed their
 closed tent full of Off!
Looking rested as they lounge in their polished cotton shorts
you know they never stayed awake to think, "What
 makes those snorts?"

Something else about these pictures, wood is neatly cut
 and stacked
like it just came from some suitcase that a valet likely packed.
They're so well put together, everything is de rigueur,
telling us there are no problems with the proper clothes
 to wear.

For camping I'll hit Marshall's, better yet, some surplus store
with cheap and rough-hewn clothing from some long
 outdated war.
Oh, I'll still shop their catalogues, I'll still make that call
to buy their smashing outfits I wear hiking through the mall.

Cappuccino by the Sea

She lives in a land of the evenly tanned
   by the edge of a golden sea
where the warm sun streams and brings grand dreams,
   the supply runs endlessly.
Here dreams are spun for everyone
   to weave a magic spell,
and fortunes are there for those who will dare
   spin those dreams into products that sell.
Each wants a piece of this golden fleece
   to charge an exorbitant rate,
for brokered dreams and exotic schemes
   are this land's business bait.
Here where value is based on fee
only consciousness is free,
in Cappuccino by the Sea.

Her glittering hair catches many a stare
   as she swirls her golden mane,
and every few weeks she gets new blonde streaks
   (it's a sin to be thought of as plain)
at a hair boutique that is currently chic
   from a young man's flashing wands,
the tools of his trade for which he's well paid
   (his name is Armando or Hans).
Thus she believes (and also deceives)

through the woven gold in her hair
she'll create the veneer for her chosen career
   so in part of the dream she can share.
For she lives in this magical place, you see,
where dreams beget plush imagery
in Cappuccino by the Sea.

She follows those laws which don't allow flaws
   nor bodies not perfect of mold.
Her workout routine keeps her form tight and lean
   like goddesses of old.
Of age there's less fear if at least once each year
   she submits to the surgeon's blade
so she lives out her life with the help of his knife
   knowing her parts look well made.
Then she can wear with a toss of blonde hair
   those dazzling new fashion designs
while she looks young and fresh as she bares her tight flesh
   with no trace of dread aging signs.
For Age, not Death, is the enemy;
arrested youth will always be
in Cappuccino by the Sea.

She acts as a sage on concepts New Age.
   It's all part of her mating dance,
done at beaches and bars through use of the stars
   and crystals and incense and chants.

"It's our ordained right to share in the light,"
   she says to each man she's just met.
She tells each new love it's decreed from above
   and she speaks of karmic debt.
She thinks their souls fuse while their bodies they use
   (to do any less is to fail),
and she's so disappointed when men thus anointed
   aren't gods from beyond the veil.
They see the light as they want it to be
while they writhe in synchronicity
in Cappuccino by the Sea.

But living in light requires insight,
   not readily found here it seems.
Those freely seduced are quickly induced
   to chase their bewitching dreams.
She lives out her days in chimerical haze
   she would never see as a hell,
nor has she a clue that no one breaks through
   her glossy crafted shell.
When dreams are begun from rays of the sun
   those dreams must all be fulfilled
but one can't be perfected if outer-directed,
   by gods through the eons we're milled.
But here, of course, she is always free
to be not all that she can be
in Cappuccino by the Sea.

Drug *Du Jour*

Today the care in mental health
generates a growth in wealth
for pushers of the sleek brochure
who tout their latest drug du jour.

They tell us that a psychic wound
means chemistry must be retuned.
They exorcise our inner devils
manipulating our blood levels.

But what of their dispersal arm,
the shrinks, do they feel no alarm
that no one now pulls up a chair
to sit with patients in despair?

Insurance pays for mega-doses
for depression or psychosis,
not to probe or delve below—
just patch them up and out they go!

People drug-stitched 'round the edges
feeling hopeless jump off ledges.
Does anyone now seek a cure,
or just the latest drug du jour?

Everybody was Surprised

She huddled 'neath her covers
with her blankets pulled up tight.
Her head and face were covered,
still she'd feel the shaft of light
each time he cracked her door
and sneaked into her room at night.

He'd pull her covers back,
then he'd start to stroke her hair.
He'd tell her how she helped him
how her mother didn't care.
She only could survive
pretending that she wasn't there.

He told her this was loving,
what he did with her was good
but she must never tell
for she would be misunderstood
and then she would be punished.
Thus, he stole her childhood.

He stopped his nightly visits
when she first began to bloom,
when seeds he left could grow

within her adolescent womb.
Instead he stole his way
into her little sister's room.

She met a boy who liked her.
As he softly stroked her hair
he said he would protect her,
said how much he'd always care.
She never told her secret
to him for she didn't dare.

They ran away and married
and she never once suspected
he, too, had a secret
which like hers went undetected
so neither of them could be
what the other one expected.

He first beat her roughly
just before their daughter's birth.
It hurt her very deeply
and destroyed her little worth.
She despaired if she could ever
find a haven on this earth.

They had another child;
she adjusted to her fate

of trying to appease him,
to not make him so irate.
The gates of hell then opened
when their oldest girl turned eight.

He would leave their bedroom
for a while most every night.
Trying not to wake her
he would not turn on a light,
still she knew where he was going,
knowing well her daughter's plight.

She lay there in her darkness
curled tightly in a ball
as helpless as her daughter.
She withdrew into this pall,
lying there for hours
mutely staring at the wall.

He called the paramedics
telling them that for a week
she barely moved at all,
in fact she didn't even speak.
The conclusion was depression
coming to some kind of peak.

They took her to a psych ward.
She'd no voice for her complaints;
she struck at them in terror
so they slapped her in restraints.
They shot her full of meds
and in O.T. they gave her paints.

Perhaps she would have spoken
if but one had seemed to care,
but staff were all so busy,
never once pulled up a chair
to quietly just sit
to be with her, with her despair.

Those who'd spoken for her
through her life had always lied.
Her own weak voice was useless
so she never really tried.
That's why she made it happen,
why she and her children died.

At home she felt too helpless
to protect them from their fate,
that prison made of incest
and, in fact, she was too late.
The only out she saw
was lead them now to heaven's gate.

She met them after school
and took them to a seaside park
for games up near the harbor bridge
to spot dolphins or a shark.
Then grasping them quite firmly
plunged them into waters dark.

Her husband claimed he'd lost
a wife and children he had prized.
The experts through the press
then had the whole thing analyzed.
Here's the grand conclusion—
everybody was surprised.

We Women Will Take Charge From Here

We women Boomers found our voices
and used them to demand new choices.
So what was our most trendy cause?
We blew the lid off menopause.
As we approached becoming crones
we didn't speak in same hushed tones
as did our mothers of "the change,"
who made sure they were out of range
of their partners, children, too.
To speak of "it" just wouldn't do.

There is no more protected ground
where women's topics can't be found.
In quiet corners, open air
we talk about them everywhere.
There are answers that we seek
so it's important that we speak
of our types of hot flash surges
and our waxing/waning urges.

At first our doctors didn't know
that estrogen made bad things grow.
They didn't have much to discuss
as they threw estrogen at us,

derived from urine of a horse
that's changed in labs through arcane course
so it became as pure, pristine
as if we're drinking gasoline.
"Just take the estrogen or not—"
the only bullet that they've got.
So we defected at this juncture,
to herbalists or acupuncture.

You pushers from drug industries
and doctors, fading deities,
take your place in line at the rear—
we women will take charge from here.

Kill for Christ

See them proudly march along,
these soldiers of the right,
with their banners and their song
to bring the heathens light.
Hear them chant in one loud voice
as, self-inflaming, they
root out dark denizens of choice
whom they hunt down as prey.
No human life's too highly priced
for those prepared to kill for Christ.

They taunt, "no one can beat us now,
we're working for God's Son.
We must protect the fetus!" How?
The muzzle of a gun.
Their aims at times are off a peg
but they say what the hell—
just shoot them in the arm or leg,
it works almost as well.
Such joy those soldiers sacrificed
feel who shoot to kill for Christ

Beacon

When that hotly
melting part of me
blinded by desire and
no longer contained
overflows to you,
I can only crawl
my shuddering way into your arms.
My beacon through that dark heat—
the sound of your voice
stroking, calling me.

The Craftsman

When the Craftsman joins two pieces
by thrusting them in fire,
it matters not a bit to Him
if it were their desire.

Wake Up!

Long-slumbering heavy-lidded eyes,
wake up! Lift those lowered veils at once
so I may see at last for which my heart cries.

Let those long draped shades now flutter,
blinking slowly in the dazzling beckoning light
answering the ceaseless prayer my soul utters.

Heavy-lidded eyes, wake up! See that bidding Sun
bring shadowy dreams of night full force to light of day,
unveiling myriad brilliant paths all joining into one.

Armor

Written for Harold E. Hughes, former Governor and United States Senator from Iowa.

I understand your armor now,
at least better than I did before.
I used to think it was something
you put on from the outside,
like a coat.

I didn't realize the plating was interiorly fitted,
fashioned from materials used in battles
fought long ago.

I had thought your armor was
to spare you wounds;
yet now I know if any
of your wound of spirit
be covered,
the slightest blow
could fell you.

If You and I Were Angels

If you and I were angels
released from mortal caste,
would our meeting be a joy?
Could we bury pain that's passed?

Would there be unity of feeling
in the heart of astral glow
or would the aching be above
as it now is down below?

If you and I were angels
and the universe were ours
would the love I feel so deeply
be fulfilled among the stars?

Can I ever going on living
in my own time and my own sphere
without a wistful peek around
to see if you are near?

I Write

I write
for those who cannot speak
of what happened
and for those who cannot
bear to hear what happened.

Weep with me, please.
Our hot tears will melt
what is too long frozen,
buried in silence
which, now freed,
flow to the surface
to find their voices
and each other.

Then you will listen
so you can speak.
Then others will hear
and they will speak

and it will end.

Lovely Death

With each look
each touch
each stroke
I shudder and die a little more
as pieces of this world
are stripped away.
Please, let it be slowly.
I want to feel every part
of this lovely death
until there is nothing left
to bar your soul
from mine.

Grief

In the wake of mortal loss
I am the greatness kindness you will know.
I am Grief,
and I am your friend,
oh, yes, I promise you this
though you will first call me enemy,
bitterly cruel when first
I drape black and lock
the doors and windows of your soul
so you cannot escape,
cannot look out.
So filled with heaviness you'll be
that you cannot lift your head nor stand
nor try to free yourself.

You will curse me
who holds you captive,
now absent the sweet soft touch of one
whose blood once ran with yours,
so familiar, so treasured,
now gone.
And you will damn me,
screaming bitter oaths
because I will not let you out
to follow the coffin into the grave.
Though you will feel beyond

the reach of any comfort,
know you are not alone,
will never be alone,
for I cannot leave you
in total darkness.
I do not have that power.
I am only the shadow
and as you now see me
then know it is the light
that makes my aspect seen.

It is I who sits with you,
holding you in place
to sort through precious scraps and fragments
of the life together shared
now slipping through your fingers
like grains of sand
as you desperately try to patch and stitch,
make vital again that casing now used up.

When at last you can embrace
that what now brings deep pain
also travels the same path,
hand in glove,
with what once brought great joy.
Only then you will be freed
to walk out of darkness
and into the light.

The Question

"Write me a poem?" He lovingly asked.
I inwardly cringed at being so tasked;
how can I look in those eyes and explain
I will if he causes me enough pain.

Splendor

The agony when feeling dies
within a heart that bitter stays
and only sees through clouded eyes
so dark they miss the brilliant rays
of splendor born in glittering skies;
and, sadly, that is how one strays.

But those who know the myriad ways
in which the path can dip and rise
or wind in much confusing maze
to cause such pain and cruel surprise,
when splendor's shrouded in dark haze
they navigate with inward eyes.

Mortal Remains

It was bitterly cold
by the open grave,
gaping and raw as those
huddled around it.
If the priest's words
weren't comforting,
they should have been.

Not all the mortal remains
of this dearly departed—
those ashes, that dust—
went into the grave,
back to the earth.
We, the mortal remains
of this soul passed on,
slowly turned and filed
back to our cars, our lives.

If there weren't any
resurrections here today,
there could have been.

Strange Customs

Mom wants cremation to make neat
the dust of her body
now leaking life
even though those with fire
always betrayed her.
I won't be there anyway she says
and I say she so floats
on rising waters
flames will never touch her.

Dutifully, soon, I cannot free myself
from strange customs of a culture
worshipping hollow shells,
I'll take this base metal box
storing Mom's ashes
(and God knows who
else was in that oven with her)
and travel many hours to a town
I never go to anymore
to place it in a niche
in a room no one goes in
that's part of a church
I don't believe in
to be near my father
who isn't there.

But something then will grow
in that desert place.
The flames could never
touch her.

A Season Short of Time

When death approaches, shows its face, the senses
   heighten more
like autumn in the northern woods with summer's
   ripeness done,
when sumac runs like wild fire up to the forest door
where woodlands are erupting all in colors of the sun.

The skies are never deeper than just before the death
of leaves in blazing glory with each color at its prime;
it's in the chilling of the air one feels dark winter's breath
fast closing in with killing frost on a season short of time.

When at last the brilliance fades, each leaf falls to the ground
to lay beneath a falling snow that radiates soft light.
In blanketing the barren land it alters scene and sound,
and glowing quiet in the dark its light is dazzling bright.

Magic

I do wonderful things.
I perform wonderful tasks.
I stand before you
with magic in my hands
and I spin it very well.
In fact, I shall spin
just for you
anything you desire
for your pleasure.

But first let me toss it to the heavens
to gather etheric mists
of memory and vision
that will so softly filter
through your mind
and gently move inward
toward your soul.
It will pull a little at your quick
because we're making new connections,
see?
And you will call it pain
and look down, down for its source
when you should look up, up!
But my magic will teach you this
in time.

Then soon
(in time it comes to pass for all)
I'll see you balanced
high upon a moon
plucking daisies from the Sun
which you tenderly present
to outstretched aching eyes
boring up from heavier planes,
and I'll expand for galaxies
when I hear you proclaim:

"I do wonderful things.
I perform wonderful tasks.
I stand before you
with magic in my hands,
and I spin it very well . . ."

Legacy

I sit at your desk where once
your daughter, my mother,
pored over all those bills
I thought were only hers to pay.

You told me stories
of how our blood
runs through the stars,
stories my mother only
knows in dreams.

Here at that desk, now mine,
I do pay my mother's bills
in very old tender,
written with blood from the stars
flowing from my fingers
over the entire world.

The Serpent's Embrace

When at last I welcome
the crushing embrace
of the serpent's coil,
when I open my blood
willingly to its fangs,
only then can I
die joyously to the Light,
admitted at last to that final passage
so particularly guarded
by those fearsome fangs,
those relentless coils.

First Sacred Fire

In ancient days the Shaman first looked out
beyond Himself; His gaze thus made the world.
And then it was He first made sacred fire
to blaze forever hidden in first water.

He spoke a blessing, throwing high His hands
decreeing sparks from newly crackling flames
to kindle light in darkness as the stars,
the dome of night reflecting on the sea.

So everywhere He looks at night is fire
and everywhere it shines upon the water.

Where Two or More are Gathered

Within this dark and sticky clay
a spark ignited here today.
At first a blinking little spark,
it soon gleamed bright and steady in the dark.

Nearby another spark burst into flame,
but no one yet could give the fire a name
not being certain what they saw—
though all of heaven was, bowing down in awe.

Beltane's Embers

Each year we see the mighty Hunter slip down western skies
as in the east again the Great Bear starts to make his rise.
It's in this magic season when the days once more grow long
I feel anew the stirring of a sacred inner song.
In shadows of the past emerging deep from cycling moons
again I hear the summons of revered and hallowed tunes,
their arcane magic echoing in me through ancient soil
that heat and churn my insides 'til my blood begins to boil.

No drum would summon them this night
to draw them to the fireside's light,
but just the boiling blood inside
from heat of rising summer tide.

When life again arises after bitter winter's spent
before ripe summer comes this call to gathering is sent:
to slip away when daylight first begins to fade and wane,
to leave the flocks and fertile fields that sprout anew with grain,
to come from lakes and winding streams that flow 'neath wooded bowers
impelled by rapture surging through the elemental powers
now calling all to festival through village, farm and hedge
to fall to earth and join anew at Beltane's fiery edge.

To sacred hilltops high and steep
the ancient rituals they keep;
wild dancers writhing to and fro
around the firelight's mounting glow.

This always builds within me at this same time ev'ry year
when we who've known the god and goddess to the fires
   draw near.
Still now I hear those voices, see the priest and priestess go
to light once more those sacred flames while passions start
   to grow.
The sun tide flows again much as artesian waters course
and as it fills and floods me I pay homage to its source.
Then all life throbs in unison in rhythm with the earth
while frenzy and mad ecstasy are midwives to rebirth.

Could those be coiling on your wrists
two serpents born in ancient mists
with firelight glinting from their eyes
whose rays seek those who seek the wise?

Was it betimes with sun tide's heat that you first took
   my hand?
Was it then long ago when other worships filled the land
long before the bishops, the iron hand of Rome,
with cross of blood as banner then inquested each
   man's home

by telling black-clad clergy that they all must search to find
then rout the sacred places where the serpents coil and wind?
The bishops drove the goddess out from home and out of bed
denying men and women ancient ways they joined and wed.

But we who've joined by Beltane's embers
it is thus that each remembers,
both the god and goddess voices
and in that knowledge each rejoices.

Star Catcher

It tugged at her, that ancient call,
so she slipped from her barren bed
   where her sisters in black were asleep
to that magical night to catch stars soon to fall.

She ran through the trees to the open space,
she flew over crests of the hills;
   with joy she embraced those fiery streaks,
their burning caresses, their kiss on her face.

All night long she danced with that Light,
wrapped in its numinous arms;
   her blood ran white and hot with its fire
forever kindling her soul in the night.

Her days were cold in those walls of stone,
sorting the dried and withered fruit,
   sifting dead ashes scorched by the Sun
while her sisters knelt silently weeping alone.

But at night she bathed in those radiant beams;
her hands still covered with silvery dust
   stroked the burning kiss on her skin
and wild she ran with the stars in her dreams.

Science Wasn't There That Night

On a clear night science says the human eye
only sees two thousand stars unaided,
but science didn't rule the night I saw the sky
blaze with a brilliance memory hasn't faded.

Millions of stars across the heavens glittered and danced;
in pulsing flashing rhythms a few would break,
fiery streaks to the edge of the sky—I watched entranced—
then plunge to earth to land behind the lake.

Even loons were silent as if in homage due.
Deep in that night while all the others slept
I softly stole out on the lake in my canoe
then lay down looking up and simply wept.

Star Pools

Like little woodland pools we are
each large enough to reflect one star,
its mirrored veil in darkest night
spiraling back to its source of light.

Like little inlets, bays are we,
part of a greater, infinite sea
where we abide behind our eyes,
where blazing stars wear no disguise.

The Visit

An intergalactic committee arrived
a while ago to see how we've thrived
down through the ages and eons and such.
Have we learned little or have we learned much?
It was quite an impressive assemblage I hear.
(In their visit to us could they find a peer?)
They came to conduct their form of reviewing
how all the kingdoms of life here are doing.

Their first stop on earth was high in the air
where only the birds are able to dare
to fly in magnificent skies all alone
(although they are losing their shielding ozone).
Are birds worried now since science revealed
the air ceased to act for the earth as a shield
the committee asked the birds frankly?
"What air?" the birds queried and stared at them blankly.

Next stop on their visit was to every ocean
to talk with the fish about the commotion
by those who agreed with and those who refuted
the claims that the oceans now are polluted.
Concerns had been raised that so much miasma
in water would damage the high food chain's plasma
when foods from the oceans were served up and fried.
"What water?" the fish in confusion replied.

Next, they proceeded to burrow in earth
where so many life forms are given birth,
to check our foundations and all the plants' shoots
from worms who were aerating all of their roots.
Didn't the worms object to the taste
of the increasing poisons from our toxic waste
and weren't they afraid that the soil now caused cancer?
"What soil?" the puzzled worms gave as their answer.

The committee's last stop was to spend time with us,
which wasn't too easy since we made a fuss
when questioned when we'd make good use of our magic
to clean up conditions they saw that were tragic
which we had created in earth, skies and ponds
by collectively using our magic wands
for selfishly hoarding what should have been shared.
"We've no magic wands!" we hotly declared.

The intergalactic committee departed
with reports on our status noted and charted:
"All lower species (well, lower than man)
seem to be living according to plan.
Of humans, of course, we'll be more enthused
when they stop getting spirit and matter confused
by thinking that of the two matter is stronger
they draw out their sentences, making them longer."

Guardianship of the Light

I, Aries, am the Light always rising in the east, a blazing path into each new dawn for others to follow.

I, Taurus, catch the Light as it touches earth to make fire in the mud that nourishes all new growth.

I, Gemini, seek each intersection of the Light, every divide, for there are always choices and all paths must be explored.

I, Cancer, nourish in my womb the quickening by Light of each seed conceived in all unions.

I, Leo, radiate Light from the heart of every matter as freely as a child gives love.

I, Virgo, carry in my hands the sacred Light that nurtures each grain of wheat, each tiny seed, for they must be perfectly ripe before being offered as flour for the bread.

I, Libra, witness the Light in all its extremities, and no matter what its distance or destination I give testimony to its one source.

I, Scorpio, bear the Light into the darkest regions that all fear but all must know, and when at last they know, they carry the Light into every death.

I, Sagittarius, soar high in screamingly ecstatic blazing dissolution into the dying of the Light.

I, Capricorn, use my stone walls to guard the flickering spark of Light burning at its lowest point so it may thrive to climb to its highest destiny.

I, Aquarius, know Light must be freed from every prison to illumine the lamp of knowledge in every mind.

I, Pisces diffuse the Light throughout the depths of my sea, leaving no drop of water in total darkness.

I'd Like to Know
(Written for my best friend, Hatheway Brooks, who walked this earth with me for 61 years)

I'll tell you what I'd like to do
the next time we're together,
just the two of us—let's share pain.
Maybe not quite what you had in mind?

OK, tightening the field a little more,
let's keep it to those moments
ushered in by print or paint or form or musical note—
not what excited or impressed us
or turned us on so we start babbling.
That can get bogus real fast.

Instead, let's share what wounded, stabbed,
caused such deep rearrangement
we were robbed of expression,
momentarily suspended in time
no matter where we were.
Then let's bring those pieces—
actually our experiences of them—
to share with each other.

Oh, I know
this violates a lot of people's notions,
including mine,
about experience and how we can't re-create The Moment
to foist on others
expecting them to feel the same.
Let's be more like William Blake
challenging us not to be one
who "binds to himself a joy..."
but to be one who "kisses the joy as it flies. . ."

Let's try it,
and if what you bring doesn't do it for me,
so what?
It would move me deeply to know
what does it for you.
So what would you bring?
I'd like to know.

I'd bring writing mostly,
starting with my favorite poet,
William Butler Yeats, and how his creations
help us see, make us feel
what binds us to our seen and unseen worlds.

I'd also bring Dostoevsky's "Notes from the Underground"
which at an early age held a mirror
to my personal "disease of excessive consciousness"
so I could begin to know it not
as something that sets me apart
but more like a prize,
something that adds to my consciousness.

Then I'd bring Lincoln's "Second Inaugural Address,"
in which I realized the Civil War (most wars in fact)
brought no real victories,
just new flags and uniforms emerging later
disguising the same ugliness as before.

I wouldn't bring just whole pieces either—
yes, let's break all the rules:
The second verse of Matthew Arnold's "The Buried Life;"
lines 1-21 of "The Hound of Heaven" by Francis Thompson.
Then there'd be "Preface to the New Translation" of Elie
    Wiesel's "Night;"
though once you turn a few pages
you'll probably read the entire book.
I'd weep when reading,
I know, because I always do—
from both fullness and sadness.

I'd have to include Charles Bukowski
because every poem and novel he wrote
that I read—and there are many—
taught me humor is birthed in hell,
and knowing that has opened many
new fields of perspective.

And music.
I'd have to include music:
Leonard Cohen's "Hallelujah" and "Joan of Arc"
(not sung by the composer—sorry, Leonard),
all things Stevie Nicks,
Samuel's Barber's "Adagio for Strings,"
and songs I learned at camp
that can still make me cry today.

I'd have to include sculpture
though I never really got sculpture
until a few years ago
when a piece got me:
Rodin's "Burghers of Calais,"
still as big and heavy in my heart
as the day I stood weeping beside it in a freezing rain,
seeing in it both the best and worst
of the human condition.

If some of your moments were
in famous museums far from here,
I could close my eyes and
I know you'd find a way
to paint the experience in my mind
so I'd see it.
Maybe this way we could sneak in
and bring to form
the essence of moments
not yet recognized by us
in print or stone or paint or tone.
For me that would be about capturing
deeply buried shadows
for which there are still no images.

So what would you bring?
I'd like to know.

I know that with us together
at times there would be tears
but also a lot of laughter.
Pain doesn't have to be sad.
It can be, but not this way.
What truly would be sad
would be if we had nothing to bring.

But that could never happen—
Not with us.

Wags

When someone falls in love with someone others think
   they shouldn't,
it's just because the others think if it were they,
   they wouldn't.
They wag their fingers cluck their tongues at how some
   people sever
ties that bind with decent folks to cleave to one who never
would be one with whom they'd choose to join with in
   great passion,
as if a fated love were found in shops like some hot fashion.

When someone falls in love with someone friends don't
   think they should have
it's not because there was a choice or not as if they
   could have.
When someone starts on someone else's love trysts in a rage
they should take note of us who on this subject
   won't engage
for when someone says it's risky, that they'd never take
   that chance,
I know for sure they've never had a partner for that dance.

Low, Slow Fire

There is a low, slow fire
burning in us all,
given to some, stolen by others,
or so it is believed by many.

The fire is real.
How it got there—well,
that's a story most don't believe
though there are clues for those
with eyes for more than seeing.

Those who smugly claim
they are gifted,
and those who steal to heal wounds
in themselves and others
miss this truth:
One can neither hoard nor steal
what burns inside another,
for what burns in one
so blazes in us all.

Qlippoth*

Shells of the dead
half live behind my mind
with just enough vitality
to be dangerous.

Those aging icons
I buried with great pomp
are now resurrected
by the drift of my shifting focus,
filling their hollowness
with essences stolen
from today's dreams.

I'm breathing life into corpses,
animating the dead.

* Hebrew for "shells of the dead."

Heliotropism

Flowers lift their faces
to seek the Sun above,
then fill with water
when the heavens rain,
bowing their heads
to spill the fullness
they cannot contain
onto the freshly growing garden
where something new and lovely
will remain.

It's a Stretch with Beagles

When Mother Nature gave us frogs,
raccoons, gazelles and eagles,
she really did her best with dogs
but it's a stretch with beagles.

They track the rabbit where it roams
and tally-ho the hunt to,
but while they're living in our homes
they do what they damn want to.

Kitchen Helpers

When entertaining I abhor
to drop food on the kitchen floor.
But if it "thumps" it doesn't matter
quite as much as some big "splatter."
"Thumps" I scoop up like a ball
and hope nobody saw at all.
"Splatters" though go everywhere
under table, stove and chair.
That's when it's my rotten luck
to have my guests come in and cluck
if through the kitchen they are crossing.
Guests are very good at bossing:
"Quick! Sponges for the countertop!"
"Too late! We need to get a mop!"

But I don't need help to decide.
I just call the dogs inside.
Two happy gluttons, in they bound
and lap the floor of all they've found.
"That's good enough for now," I say,
"so let's go eat and drink and play.
I'll wash the floor when we're all through."
But then, of course, I never do.

Double-shot Ambience

City night, coffee place,
thrill us with a brand new taste.

"A double-shot no foam double-cup latte tall."
More useless merchandise stacked along the wall.

Bump patter bump patter bump bump patter bump.

"A decafe no whip double-shot mocha tall?"
"No no no no!
A double-shot no foam double-cup latte tall."

Road trip, down the road,
gotta go, let it rip.

No one there was sober,
sucking up a toke or two;
the rhythm taking over,
snaking through the smoke it knew
where to thread its roadway through the neon aisles.

Looking for some light, that coiling spark
dodging greasy hands, slick oily smiles.
Listen to that back door alley way dog bark.

"A straight up ice-cold double-shot vodka here,
put it in my hands now.
Let me drink it down. How?
Put it where I'm lying here.
Take some money off the bar, buy yourself a beer."

The rhythm's pounding harder, getting strong,
beating on the inside, a brand new under-song.
"Shut it out! Close us down and lock the door!
I don't want to dance here anymore!"

Got to, have to find some place to hide.
The last safe place? Got to get outside!
That river in the dull sky, hot with fire,
burns new holes in the night of old desire.

The map is not the territory.
The map is not the territory.
The rhythm knows the roadway.
The rhythm knows the roadway.

So grab those fiery currents by their tails,
both feet riding on the double hot rails;
careen down dark-rimmed canyons of the sun
where all the untamed wild creatures run.

A keening, screaming terrifying ride
and when it's done
you're back inside
where no one needs that double-cup load—
just one black coffee for the road.

Come on Down the Road

You built yourself a dream house
with care, style and great planning;
most of all you built it with love
and you live in it with love, for the moment.
But don't you see?
It's all used up now.
It's time to move on
for the joy of love is in the building
not in the residing.

So come! Come on down the road.
Let someone else move in,
someone who could use the touch of your soul
you so tenderly included in every piece.
For you became strong
when you found you were a builder.
Don't let your talents fade—

Come! Come on down the road.
There are so many dreams to be built
with you the designer,
building them for so many others
who need dreams to live in
as they come on down the road.

Prayer of a Communicant

This is my body
with holes punched in it
all the way to my soul.
This is my blood
running with too many others' blood
spilling darkly from secret places
most refuse to see
to this ritual ground where I now kneel
slimy with memories.

The pieces of your body offered
look so puny,
but slowly your body grows patches in mine
one thin wafer at a time
weaving repairs as fine as spider webs
and strong, so strong.

When I could not drink from your cup,
the cup you offered
to show me the difference
between them and you,
you worked a miracle for me
changing wine into water
which, kneeling before my reeling body,

you gently poured over my hair
still sticky and tangled with blood.
Using your fingers as a comb
you tenderly and thoroughly washed it away
until finally I could look in your eyes and drink.

Sadly, I've come to know
that when the world view is filled
with bodies blown to pieces,
the carnage laid end to end for miles
so it cannot be denied,
it still will be denied.
The world does not see, will not see
it is you who gathers the bodies,
the slain with their slayers.
It is you who stitches
their ragged memories,
who washes blood and revenge
from their vision,
who feeds them all from your body's bounty
providing whatever nourishment
will help them remember
when later they awake in your arms
that they are whole,
that they are yours,
that you are so much larger
than any religion claims to define you.

Let me eat so I can help.
Let me walk with you
through the gory battlefields
I survived.
Those already dead are yours
but the wounded who wander dazed
just now waking
to the shock and horror
are mine.
They need someone
to wash the blood away,
the ones too injured to call to you,
too numb to care if you are there.
They need one who, too, survived the battle
they both know,
to sit with them
through the long pain-filled nights ahead.

This is my body.
May it live only to serve.
This is my blood.
It already runs with yours,
flowing through the same great heart.

The Canoe

Today I looked longingly at this canoe.
Its color was an evening gray in tone;
it was beached where the whole lake was in view
beyond which pine edged rivers ran alone.

A single paddle rested on the bow
inviting me. How easy just to go
a week or two, I'd work it out somehow,
down waters where the northern sun hangs low.

I wouldn't need to have a map or guide.
I've done it all before. I'd quickly find
my way through wooded waterways and glide
through passages I've kept within my mind.

My sense of joy exceeded any name...
then daydreams snapped—I wouldn't go at all.
The canoe I saw was trapped in paint and frame,
pressed 'neath glass and hanging on a wall.

Through Eyes About to Die

My first night in that valley at the ranch there was no moon,
yet still the peaks were glowing with a dusty silver hue.
My breath came out in wintry clouds though it was early June
as dazzling starlight cast the valley all in whitish blue.
Not far away I heard the rhythm of a creek untamed;
coyotes howling in the night sent chills down to the bone.
Then beneath the starlight moved a shadow yet unnamed
and standing in its darkness I felt utterly alone.
Though all the other mountains 'round the valley gleamed
  with light,
that mountain just behind me towered darkly in the night.

My first day at the ranch the mountains were a startling sight
with sunlight blazing brightly off each rocky craggy face
as if the eerie shadow shrouding me the previous night
were some nocturnal creature that bright sunlight could erase.
Yet shadowy impressions still were sifting through my mind
as pungent to my senses as the mountain flowers and sage.
But I ignored these feelings and for years left them behind,
for at the ranch that day I was just thirteen years of age.
Adventures with my horse and friends I had three
  summers there
would keep at bay for years that mountain's secret I
  would share.

One day on horses racing to some adolescent dare,
we crashed through stands of aspens and across a crystal creek
into a tiny clearing where we found in disrepair
a graveyard hidden in the shadow of that mighty peak.
There twenty rotting wooden markers gave a strange report
that all those buried there had died some decades long before
within a few months' span, no clue why lives had been
   cut short,
or why no men, just women and the children that they bore.
The filtered sunlight cast the graveyard all in dappled gold;
In spite of mountain summer heat I suddenly felt cold.

When we are young and apperceive events too big to hold,
they go across some bridge in time to where our futures grow,
and when their times are ripe their full-grown stories
   will unfold.
But on that day astride my horse with all those graves below,
I sat there frozen in my saddle very close to tears
while others milled about the graves, called out each name
   and date.
My horse was standing quietly though flies buzzed 'round
   his ears
as if like I he couldn't move, trapped in some unclaimed fate.
I only saw three graves that day — they held me like a snare,
a woman and two children; I was numb, could only stare.

She died a few days after both her children were laid there.
The markers on those graves were taller and the writing clearer,
as if the one who marked them had some message to declare.
I had no way of knowing then these graves were some
   strange mirror.
We never found out who they were or how they all had died;
we asked around in town but those we asked seemed not
   to know.
We might have found the answer if persistently we'd tried,
but we were young with more adventures yet to undergo.
My teenage focus wandered far away from those grave sites
until in years to come they'd visit me in quiet nights.

I never went back to those graves, I never scaled the heights
up on that mountain by the ranch, though all the others had.
Those summers there were glorious but sometimes in
   those sights
I'd see that towering peak and I'd feel deeply sad.
I don't know when they surfaced first from deep beneath
   my mind,
those memories extending far beyond which I could know.
At night as I would go to sleep this image I would find—
that mountain just behind the ranch all covered up
   with snow.
I only spent the summers there so I did not know why
I saw that peak in winter, saw through eyes about to die.

She knew when all the others fell what she could not deny.
She dug graves in late autumn just before the rocky ground
froze too hard for digging. For her children she must try
to give a resting place for after snow they'd not be found.
Resigned by winter's eve the three of them would not be spared,
she tore three sturdy planks out of a now abandoned stall.
She wanted those who came behind to know someone had cared;
at night by fire's edge she carved their names on markers tall.
They died her precious children, those to whom she'd given birth,
and swaying weak with fever she then laid them in the earth.

Now did it happen neatly? What's this tragic story's worth?
What if we went back to their graves and dug them up today?
Was there much more transpired that we need to now unearth,
and might we find there are no bones there lying in decay?
What if what really happened was as winter lashed its snows,
she was alone and dying and as anyone would dread
she'd be too weak to feed her children, kiss their ears and toes.
There'd be no one to care for them when she was cold and dead.
There was no moon the night they died, that mountain
   loomed up high
as starlight sparkled on the snow and danced across the sky.

She told them magic stories for the wolves' howls made them cry.
She waited for approaching night, made sure the fire was spent,
then told her children down that mountain angels soon would fly
to fold them warmly in their wings, so watch for their descent.
She took them from the cold dark hearth to lead them to their death

and held them close and kissed them as she ushered them outside;
They thought they saw the angels hover through each cloudy breath
as lying in the snow together looking up they died.
That mountain like a headstone was the last thing that she saw.
The coyotes kept her secret from exposure in spring's thaw.

Now some would rail with fervor at her sin, her deadly flaw;
still others would extol that she was brutal or insane.
If she applied to heaven she'd be hurled into hell's maw.
Still others would defend her deed as loving and humane.
Such acts live unremittingly in hollows of the soul
like sand within an oyster long before the pearl grows.
They fester deep in memory not letting us feel whole
until the pain of secret deeds seeks light and must disclose.
It's then a shadow covers us some dazzling starry night
that clouds our lives with darkness forcing us to find the light.

There is a feeling carried deep against which women fight,
that earth to which we bear our children claims them all
   too soon,
and locked within this ancient fray resist that their birthright
will be they're taken from us in some dark phase of the moon.
The night I lost my child that was yet unborn to me,
again, I saw that mountain looming silent, white and cold.
Finally I saw what it was telling me to see,
so in my pain its troubling secret finally was told—
to see me as a mother now would happen no way save
that time I sat upon my horse and looked on my own grave.

When I Am Old

When I am old if I could have a place,
a quiet little place where I could sit
and look on water edged with pines and firs,
with oaks and birches clustered in the sand
and clinging bravely to the rocky shores.
If I could see the evening's fading light
as it pours melted copper on the water,
its afterglow that filters through the boughs
of spiring trees that shelter where I sit.
If I could see across to other shores
(You see, I'd have to see the other shores,
the world I'd live in would be smaller then.)
I'd see the gentle contours of the hills there
all crowned with forests thick with ancient timber,
my theater to watch the constant play
of light and shadows weaving fluid patterns
throughout the day and into falling night. . .
then it would be enough, when I am old.

When I am old, so old that most with whom
I've shared the richness of my life are gone,
if I could have a little place on water,
a sanctum on some crystal bay or cove
from where I'd see the rising moon reflecting

on the gently rippled surface of the bay.
And when it's dark if I could see a light
that glimmers now and then from down the shore,
just one or two to know I'm not alone. . .
then it would be enough, when I am old.

When I am old if I am fated so,
as is my mother and I cannot see,
I still would want my little place on water
where I could always hear the steady lap
of waves upon the shore, and also hear
the quiet whispering of wind through pines,
the supple birches whipping in the breeze.
There'd be the mournful, eerie wails of loons
that haunt the night, the splash a hungry fish
makes leaping out of water hunting flies.
I would not need to see the coming storm,
I'd smell it in the air and feel its coolness,
its dampness on my skin; I'd hear the rhythm
of rising wind that makes the wild waves,
their frenzied rapid slapping on the rocks. . .
Then it would be enough, when I am old.

When I am old if fortune leaves me poor
and I can't have my place that rests near water,
if I could then be brought to this retreat

for just a while by some kind kindred soul,
I'd like to be alone and given time,
just time enough to share in my exchange
that I so need there with that bit of water
to fill up like a brimming cup to hold
and carry with me through my final passage. . .
then it would be enough, when I am old.

The Temple

He was a traveler, explorer
who ran out of destinations.
He had traveled to a village
in a land where all the maps
and all his comrades told him
held no treasure;
still, he found he could not leave.

His heart was very restless
for he had no destination.
Like a wild creature caged
he daily paced the market
and at night he scanned the stars.

One morning in the village
came an old one to his side who said,
"You have a destination."
Then he thrust a glowing golden key
into his eager hands.

"Begin at dawn, walk toward the sun.
You'll know when you've arrived."
And then the old one vanished
in the din of market bustle.

The man was an explorer;
he now had a destination,
so he started out at dawn
and he walked into the sun.
The way was thick with jungle
that tore harshly at his clothes.
Sharp branches cut his skin
but he clutched that golden key,
and his steps though slow were steady.

The jungle fell away
and standing there before him
was an ancient temple door
with a lock of burnished gold.
He fitted tremblingly his key
and the door swung open wide.

He stood within the portal
where a softly spreading light
from a source he could not see
washed through him and around him,
and the jagged edges of his life
at once turned smooth as stone.
He dropped down to his knees
with his arms stretched out before him.
His tears were flowing freely,
face pressed hard upon the floor.

Devotedly and slowly
he kissed each and every stone
for they fit perfectly together.
He blessed the quarry master
who had cut free every stone;
he blessed the grand designer,
blessed the builders who had fitted
every stone within this temple,
and he blessed this holy place.

Then he could lift his eyes at last
and know he, too, was holy.
He saw that at the altar
was a company of those
who had walked the path before him,
who like him lost destination,
who had struggled through the jungle
clutching hard their golden keys,
who arriving torn and bleeding
fell upon their knees and wept,
had blessed and kissed each stone
on their way up to the altar.

In one clear voice they told him
and he knew their words were true:
"Only the Invited Ones
can ever enter here."

They then opened up their body
and received him in their light.

With his new collective vision
he could see beyond the walls.
On the path that he had traveled
walking blindly toward the sun,
a traveler advanced.
The jungle tore his clothes apart,
sharp branches cut his skin,
but he tightly clutched his golden key.
His steps were slow but steady.

From deep within the altar
this body made of light
reached out lovingly to touch
that tortured, tired traveler
at last to bring him home.

THANK YOU FOR READING MY BOOK!

Dear Reader,

I hope you enjoyed *Wit, Snark, and Light in the Dark*.

As an author, I value getting feedback. I would love to hear what your favorite poem was, and what you liked or disliked, please share your thoughts with me. You can write me at dsparies@gmail.com.

Also, I'd like to ask a favor. If you are so inclined, please write a review of *Wit, Snark, and Light in the Dark* on Amazon and Goodreads. You, the reader, have the power to influence other readers to share your journey with a book you've read. In fact, most readers pick their next book because of a review or on the advice of a friend. So, please share! You can find all of my books on my Amazon author page.

Thank you so much for reading *Wit, Snark, and Light in the Dark* and thanks for spending time with me and my poems.

Best regards,

Deborah Smith Parker

About the Author

Deborah Smith Parker grew up bilingual, fluent in both prose and poetry. Beginning at an early age she learned from her father to compose rhythmic, and rhyming verse. She also learned from him about the stars, the constellations, and the myths that connected them.

Her poems, essays and articles have appeared in a wide range of published outlets ranging from *Journal of the American Medical Association* to *The Mountain Astrologer* to *North County Times* to *Nuthouse* to *New Press Literary Quarterly*, winning some prizes along the way.

An English major and graduate of the University of Wisconsin-Madison, Parker lives in San Diego with her husband Jeff.

www.ingramcontent.com/pod-product-compliance
Lightning Source LLC
Chambersburg PA
CBHW030945090426
42737CB00007B/544